To:

Love From:

Measurement Conversion Chart

Imperial	Metric	Cups
1/2 Fl.oz	15ml	1 Tablespoon
1 Fl.oz	30ml	1/8 Cup
2 Fl.oz	60 ml	1/4 Cup
4 Fl.oz	125ml	1/2 Cup
5 Fl.oz (1/4 pint)	150ml	2/3 Cup
6 Fl.oz	175 ml	3/4 Cup
8 Fl.oz	250 ml	1 Cup
12 Fl.oz	375 ml	1.1/2 Cup
16 Fl.oz	500 ml	2 Cups

Tablespoon	Teaspoon
1	3
2	6
4	12
6	18
8	24
10	30
12	36

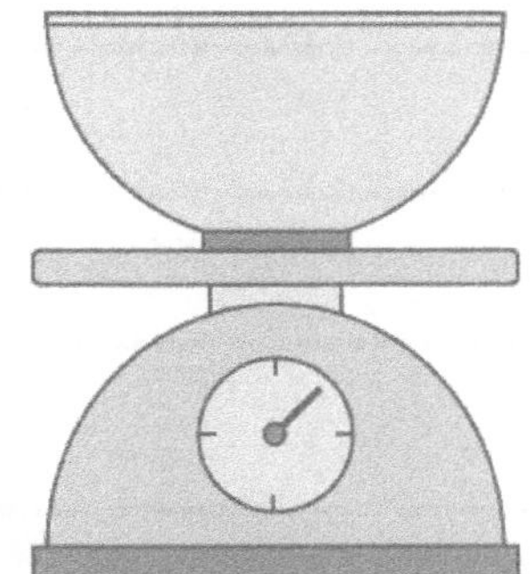

Recipe:

Ingredients List:

Prep Time:

Cooking time:

Serves:

Rating:

★★★★★

Equipment List:

Instructions:

Recipe Notes:

Family Holiday Traditions:

Memories to Share:

Notes and Keepsakes:

Recipe:

Ingredients List:

Prep Time:

Cooking time:

Serves:

Rating:

★★★★★

Equipment List:

Instructions:

Recipe Notes:

Family Holiday Traditions:

Memories to Share:

Notes and Keepsakes:

Recipe:

Ingredients List:

Prep Time:

Cooking time:

Serves:

Rating:

★★★★★

Equipment List:

Instructions:

Recipe Notes:

Family Holiday Traditions:

Memories to Share:

Recipe:

Ingredients List:

Prep Time:

Cooking time:

Serves:

Rating:

★★★★★

Equipment List:

Instructions:

Recipe Notes:

Family Holiday Traditions:

Memories to Share:

Recipe:

Ingredients List:

Prep Time:

Cooking time:

Serves:

Rating:

★★★★★

Equipment List:

Instructions:

Recipe Notes:

Family Holiday Traditions:

Memories to Share:

Recipe:

Ingredients List:

Prep Time:

Cooking time:

Serves:

Rating:

★★★★★

Equipment List:

Instructions:

Recipe Notes:

Family Holiday Traditions:

Memories to Share:

Notes and Keepsakes:

Recipe:

Ingredients List:

Prep Time:

Cooking time:

Serves:

Rating:

★★★★★

Equipment List:

Instructions:

Recipe Notes:

Family Holiday Traditions:

Memories to Share:

Notes and Keepsakes:

Recipe:

Ingredients List:

Prep Time:

Cooking time:

Serves:

Rating:

★★★★★

Equipment List:

Instructions:

Recipe Notes:

Family Holiday Traditions:

Memories to Share:

Notes and Keepsakes:

Recipe:

Ingredients List:

Prep Time:

Cooking time:

Serves:

Rating:

★★★★★

Equipment List:

Instructions:

Recipe Notes:

Family Holiday Traditions:

Memories to Share:

Notes and Keepsakes:

Recipe:

Ingredients List:

Prep Time:

Cooking time:

Serves:

Rating:

★★★★★

Equipment List:

Instructions:

Recipe Notes:

Family Holiday Traditions:

Memories to Share:

Notes and Keepsakes:

Recipe:

Ingredients List:

Prep Time:

Cooking time:

Serves:

Rating:

★★★★★

Equipment List:

Instructions:

Recipe Notes:

Family Holiday Traditions:

Memories to Share:

Notes and Keepsakes:

Recipe:

Ingredients List:

Prep Time:

Cooking time:

Serves:

Rating:

★★★★★

Equipment List:

Instructions:

Recipe Notes:

Family Holiday Traditions:

Memories to Share:

Notes and Keepsakes:

Recipe:

Ingredients List:

Prep Time:

Cooking time:

Serves:

Rating:

★★★★★

Equipment List:

Instructions:

Recipe Notes:

Family Holiday Traditions:

Memories to Share:

Notes and Keepsakes:

Recipe:

Ingredients List:

Prep Time:

Cooking time:

Serves:

Rating:

★★★★★

Equipment List:

Notes and Keepsakes:

Recipe:

Ingredients List:

Prep Time:

Cooking time:

Serves:

Rating:

★★★★★

Equipment List:

Instructions:

Recipe Notes:

Family Holiday Traditions:

Memories to Share:

Notes and Keepsakes:

Recipe:

Ingredients List:

Prep Time:

Cooking time:

Serves:

Rating:

★★★★★

Equipment List:

Instructions:

Recipe Notes:

Family Holiday Traditions:

Memories to Share:

Notes and Keepsakes:

Recipe:

Ingredients List:

Prep Time:

Cooking time:

Serves:

Rating:

★★★★★

Equipment List:

Notes and Keepsakes:

Recipe:

Ingredients List:

Prep Time:

Cooking time:

Serves:

Rating:

★★★★★

Equipment List:

Instructions:

Recipe Notes:

Family Holiday Traditions:

Memories to Share:

Petal Publishing

CO.

Lightning Source UK Ltd.
Milton Keynes UK
UKHW051907301120
374378UK00008B/1236

9 781922 515643